STOPS

STOPS

JOEL SLOMAN

𝒵

ZOLAND BOOKS
Cambridge, Massachusetts

First edition published in 1997 by
Zoland Books, Inc.
384 Huron Avenue
Cambridge, Massachusetts 02138

"I am a tree or a dog," "Burning,"
"Every land is an improvisation," "In olden
times," and "I am a *boulevardier* in Paris"
were originally published in *WRIT*.
"Constellations" was originally published in
the *Boston Book Review*.
"Rags to Riches" and "To the Sky" were
originally published in *Exquisite Corpse*.

FIRST EDITION

Book design by Glenn Suokko
Cover illustration by Susan Shup
Printed in the United States of America

03 02 01 00 99 98 97   8 7 6 5 4 3 2 1

This book is printed on acid-free paper,
and its binding materials have been chosen
for strength and durability.

Library of Congress
Cataloguing-in-Publication Data

Sloman, Joel.
    Stops / Joel Sloman.
        p.   cm.
    ISBN 0-944072-82-8
    I. Title.
PS3569.L64S76   1997
811'.54—dc21   97-3165
                                    CIP

In memory of my sister Judy

CONTENTS

II

III

PREFACE

Joel Sloman's poems in this new book retain the unique imagination I well remember from his student days at CCNY and from his first collection, *Virgil's Machines,* which I selected for publication in 1966 by W.W. Norton, for whom I was poetry advisor at the time. If less exuberant, his work has gained in condensation in the intervening years. Often, in apparent non-sequiturs, he pushes his juxtapositions—images, perceptive flashes—close to the edge of that precipice far below which some elitist poetic clans disport themselves, forgetful that language belongs to everybody, a common good...But Sloman neither jumps nor falls over that brink: the means by which he stretches our expectations of language and continually surprises us are not erosions of grammar and syntax but swifter adjacencies than we are used to, even after decades of familiarity with the dictum, 'one perception must lead immediately to another perception' etc.

Joel Sloman (thank God) is not a "confessional" poet in the current sense; his work has a very different and more genuine candor, revealing to an unusual degree the naked movement of mind and eye among phenomena. At the same time, a nervous and (he himself claims) neurotic self-observer stands, shadowy, at the edges or in the midst of the cinematographic lines of each poem, as if disconcerted by what he notes.

All of this would, of course, be of little interest if so many of those close-packed images were not so beautiful, so rooted in the palpable, breathable world. Though his work is not 'about' description, Sloman can evoke sensory impressions with thrilling, hallucinatory precision; among them his anxious questions vanish and reappear like pilgrims wandering in an immense but enticing forest.

Denise Levertov

It rains on elms' tall pillars.
The baby's garden dwarfs its house
with golden super giant marigolds, sunflowers, and morning
    glory vines,
while water darkens for ducks of the future, superducks—
Muscovy Austro-Hungarian Byzantines.

Starlings dark, pinks on gravel.

In Nursery World, a fertile folksiness.
"Don't hang noodles on my ears!"
Some taped Xs from furious Bob's joyous welcome.
We greet you in Buzzards Bay,
throw branches on the pyre,
walk solemnly along crosswalks—along blood.
Yield!

It's all having a negative impact on me.
The purple maples—the One-Color.
Those looks, proud to be obliterating,
vacantly sloped blue shoulders, broadcasted laughter.

Uphill in poor visibility.
Shaggy limbs fall before our faces.
Espresso warps unguarded eyes.
Dark nostrils.
A monochromatic plainness pursues its individual purpose
    with unfathomable devotion.

The defiling tug on her arm is merely her headphone cord,
provoking an elegantly superior expression.

Again the back of color turns toward us.
Its spirit ages, acquires delicacy, tact, and flair,
beneath which an ideology of despair
restrains its inspiration, a harassed weed—
deity of martyred blades.

Where is the blood coming from?
A pole draped, flowers at field's far end.
The remote Tarzan's peal from fog-gelled forest.
A peak, a roof, gray and white scrim
behind performing trees.

Am I closer to thee, dotted world?
In stillness, a resolving confusion.

I throw myself out of bed with a martial arts grunt.

These black shapes, so openly disagreeing.
A pixel sails from port to port on a chip.

They are walking in wind and companionship.

Small unstoppered bottles of blue stain the lumpy cloudscape.
Strange, messy, formal things—gray, green, and bisque.
Dryly slithering in all directions and dimensions—
a haphazard wind.

"Walk-ins welcome."

Quick leaves yellow spots.

A soft streak of striated cloud above perfect blooms of
     pink, yellow, blue.
Brown eyes are put away in their plush case.

Branches straining a multitude of joints.
Maintenance-hungry yellow balusters.
Half-frozen plants.
Rose coins of leaves.
Vertiginous depth between buildings.

Am I lucky to be born in a free country?
Am I lucky to exist on this scale?

Clothes don't fit.
Policies don't fit.
They are hand-me-downs.

The destitute view is unobstructed.
"Love difference!"
I am on the downs of age.

Already a smudge, Gotham-sized bumps,
Bobcats milling, shoving asphalt, polishing an already
    featureless Earth into a bearing's selfless portraiture.

Cars signal their intentions.
Unclean, gray, problematic cloud.
It's my bullying versus its bullying, courting a majestic tree.
Boat's long upward curve to prow.

Suddenly I'm a shoe fetishist.
And within the glove—toes!

Dirty windows dull the known brightness
until the negative inside asserts itself.
Smoke, yes, but mirrors threaten morbidity and terror.
The sameness is a limited sameness.
It gradually becomes another sameness—
the bright smile, *attacca,* now churns.

Asters continue in warm microclimates.

In our love display
we are vulnerable,
but your chilliness
leaves us choiceless—
untenably for rulers.
We need wiggle room.

Once we finish, we will repeat.
There are only so many regimes,
and within is without, like knots.

We have evolved onward from some convictions,
though others are protean—
spattered silk, black ringlets, dangling ornaments.

Samples of clouds drive down the sky,
acting antically, like foreigners.
A golden beech rides in its stead.

The inheritance is speechless, but looks
through a window, squints on its crag,
like a cursed and tortured god.

The pretty blue crossed by a dust-raising herd of clouds,
dapper rifts where I was born.

My neighbors switch to Creole to discuss transvestism in
    privacy.
Thick blond hairdo sweeps forward and up, leaning
    precariously over "cryptopuzzles."

Dark maple red and maple yellow.
Tasteless spires.
Chartreuse bike.
Dried basket-like hosta stalks.
Shakes shaking on wall.
Abundant yellow berries.

Stained clothes sabotage dignity.
Is delicacy virtuous?

While an ugly green house vibrates in a pale light
     that enriches colors at our expense, her sister is dying
     in Canada.
Is it an affective disorder to be unable to comprehend any
     but logical steps?
Instead, meaning spreads from each thing like a potion
     in wine.

The house jumps from culture to culture, time to time, as does
     a face or plant.

These forms—pearls.
Yellow and black, sickly and pale.

An aging spruce's limbs flap like wide sleeves, slashed by a red
     and silver jet.
The intimacies of penmanship are replicated by frost on grass.

Shores in a teacup, an infinite coastline, the crusty edges of
     a wound.
Aiming too earnestly for something better or higher, the new
     construction miniaturizes the haunted and dilapidated
     landscape.

There is absolutely nothing above the houses—no sky.
Pre-snow white, upright poking—exploration.
Disaster of weeds.

"We were totally devastated."
"It's as if everyone was dissolved by an acid and seeped into
     the ground."
"This used to be a prosperous place."
"We don't think of ourselves as refugees."

While some lost echoes of the chorus still wander in my ear,
the Sun—in its bathrobe, humming—engrosses all.

Claire, I implore you!
This "recession kind of situation" will have to be acknowledged.
We can move forward from there.
The river and clock were frozen under the Tool and
    Equipment Rentals building,
rows of gymnosperms crushed rocks with their boots.
A barnlike roof sheltered an exotic fire.
Smooth, naked twigs toggled silvery tips.

I wrote my cards on the bus.
This is how my day went, this was my previous minute.
The year was fine—productive.
We took that turn at speed.
Our relationship has, if anything, improved.
Everything broad and flat was white, topographically like silk.

What fine design!
Worthy of twentieth-century Japanese kitsch—
"Greeting Card Sun Disk Edge
Sharpened by Charcoal-Streaked Cloud Gauze."

Gelatin River in phase indecision.
"Should I be ice? Should I be liquid?
Maybe I'll be a slushy, sloshing granité
with festive iridescent mallard topping."

Is this good for the ducks,
whose gelatinous fat insulates their blood?

A sweet smell of decay wafts through homeless air,
rising in cold, white, chrysanthemum-cloud sky.

I am a tree or a dog.

An ornate light blue grill on door we speed by.
Geese are flying in a V-formation very quietly for geese.
If you're a goose, you should honk!

We are very serious in our intention to get through this
intersection, but the red light is behaving legalistically.

I am a simple—paranoid—man.
"Beware of dog" "No trespassing"—
red-lettered signs on abundant dark brown clapboards.

Is it admirable they rise as one and fall as one?
Birds, feathery automatons.

Do I like all this reflective nodding and bowing in conversation?
Why can't I be totally unresponsive, or just plain fucking
    nonlinear?

Everyone's unique.
Why should you be different?

Gray cone of spruce.
Gulls swirl and land on flat yellow-brick rectory roof.
Yellow volumes, curlicues of limbs.
The fish weather vane points north atop doll house
as the jets curve in air
makes it seem to swoon to a vocalist's sexy eye.

Warm skies blow a pitiful nothingness, a dark parodied
    femininity, complexity tacked on each tree.
These Arabic strokes, a static-filled interlude passing through
    me, a sheet of jumbled cloud.

Its hair is never an appropriate style, so how can I tell
which degree of informality to assume?

Earrings within earrings!
As the continents turn to ocean discontinuously,
panicked, trapped weeds are never blown down only one way
    across the whole meadow.

Not quite "snow holiday"—just "holiday strictly enforced
   by snowy troops."

Hidden paths abruptly appear,
rounded features allure.
Left behind in the "emptiness shower," trees pose and listen,
   jerry rigged like the utilities' poles and cables.

United in their opposition to the central authority, my body's
   far-flung separatist district headquarters meet to plot my
   dissolution—tissue, organ, limb.

The artist selects a yard or a clump of vegetation.
A single column marches through.
Hexagonal shingles, an infield, tire track attractors.

The day starts slow—dapper fedora, a dash of color.
The gray is familiar, sanity far off.
To cope with my alienation I plunge into gestures.
Those boards are horizontal, others vertical—
there's a moral in this!

Trees show their insides in winter,
the same old spring release yet unstaged.
I'm acting in this play of hemp hair.
It's Egyptology.

The Hi-Lo's sing Kurt Weill and Langston Hughes's "Moon
     Faced, Starry Eyed" with West Coast musicians of
     the fifties.
"We would rather not be categorized," Gene Puerling writes
     in the liner notes.
Yet they are, in hindsight, notwithstanding their preferences.

I wonder about that while the frightening business of the day
grinds on—the near repetition of readings on a bathroom
     scale.
Things go up and down within a narrow range,
the boundaries of a flight path, a plane's not a gull's,
though gulls ascend in accord with the air's structure, the
     composer's notes, and a tree
leans on a house, domesticating itself.

ZURBURÁN

A bifurcation, a candelabrum—
comfortable discontinuities.
I am searching for odd and meaningful juxtapositions.
The surface noise is discouraging.

Almost Tuscan, faded lavender lilacs
toss before terra cotta. A smoky green hill
tactfully exits the landscape without drawing too much
        attention to itself.

Only the saint's left forearm is horizontal.
Everything else leads indirectly to another place,
        shifting the blame.

Ribbons are for tying her book shut,
wool tassels decorate the hippy bag over her arm,
laces hang from collar and cuffs,
black and red beads circle her neck.

More slashed sleeves.

The dragon's shriveling arabesques cringe in awe.
Streaked glass lets in today's color-hating light.

All the trees, the birds, houses, atmospheric effects, and light
live where they should, internally.
Don't just stand around!
The "No Trucks" sign is knocked askew.
Hundreds of pleasure vehicles assemble for drill.
A show by the neighborhood players advertised in the
        Styles-A-Head window.
European immigrants board the bus, naively déclassé.
Certain styles don't age, some profiles
recapitulate generations, wars, famines.
"Smile, you'll look better!"
Collectivized wisdom,
eternal village.

Unlucky sun, fairy boots.
It wrenches the world we recognize, unseeing.

Which senses organize this airy whole,
spaces of music, politics, brown, brown-yellow, brown-red,
lived-in leather, wrinkles brushing a whitening vibration of sky?
If I don't understand this standing pool,
how can I put on another volume,
shaped by its own air drying?

Rabbit teeth, sun glowing in waves of henna.

"Super Low Price"
"Foes of ex-champion ... "

Homes coyly hold trees before them like fans.

Too tired to talk politics,
the American republic vents frustrated aromatic scents.
There are no mountains here, so the sky is small.
It's "Little Sky" country.

A young woman with a precipitous profile and large nose above,
    inward-pointing knees and toes below.

Blue boxcars behind brick factory.

Two fingers support her head, one on either side of ear.
She's scrunched up, fidgety.
Her hair extends her profile in an upward sweep.

So many identical political opinions, houses, jackets.

Skirt above knees, red mouth open, arched upper lip,
she wobbles off the bus inelegantly.

I absorb greenhouse heat. It hums and whooshes.

Something flowery in the sky,
assertion displaced by seduction.
The monolithic stump is generating sprays of tendrils.
Prehistory circles its prey—
maroon pantyhose, navy blue skirt,
accidents like tilted chimneys, damp tire tracks,
a spilled liquid streaming along rubber troughs.

II

"I could curl up into a little ball and stay there."
A cat crawls out of flowering grass,
a dog rolls in weeds by church's dated cornerstone.
The river green, *pissenlits*.
Dogwood's poised salmon petals enunciate calmly.
Leaves at fewer and fewer dpi slowly dissolve spring.

My mode is evasion, her clothes summer white.

A gull swoops along a slanted parcel of air inches above a
    pointed wavelet.
It banks to let a gust pass.

A cormorant's muscular neck is a mirror-distorted, shallow
    curve.
Diving, it wriggles through a movie soundtrack of closely
    miked breath and bubbles.

The warbler's somewhere in the shrubs.

Sprinklers depopulate the landscape.
I'll steal some mulch for sweet peas.
Sweet locust's trembling crown.

A mystery plot intrudes.
Chambray shirt, culottes.
Chewing bubble gum and sage.
I tried to draw it, failed.
The right touch elusive, a lifeless scrawl.

Layered worlds—birds', ours, mine alone.
Their thoughts I'll never know.
One starling descends a step at a time,
another flaps all five.
They are both sleek, their yellow beaks open.

The Institute's public space
is filled with brown shoulders, gold jewelry—
pear-shaped loops, thread-thin chains.
A woman throws her arms around a man, embarrassing him.
A yellow flower lifts its head above the lawn,
        a sales pitch to bees.

This black-and-white spider
moves as if responding to a clicked-on power switch.
It drives all over the black-eyed Susan like a dune buggy.

A yellow one's giant pincerlike forelegs
incrementally encircle an uninvited though not unwelcome
    guest.

Her teeshirt's back flaps up,
exposing a marble spine,
arched like a cormorant's in its effortful liftoff.

The garden statues sneeze.
Spells and dreams fly back to hell.
A breeze charms popped ears.

In the Book of Abundance, routes run
the gauntlet of possibilities. So you walk the corridor,
a time-lapse dream as you undress.

The garden is infested with slugs, new flowers
lure new insects—jewels lay gems that writhe.

And I came from that too, we were closely bound.
Born with flaws predisposing us to hardy
colonies—populations—of memories.

SWEET PEA

Reflections age like the backs of palms—
wrinkled snakeskin worked leaf thin. Scared eyes
watch a weak defender with suspicion.

White sky, ageless banks, pleasure boats—
silk ribbons that mark a place in scripture.
Braces and boards grow weary of language.

A milliner's sweet pea opens its fishmouth
of pale landpink; another—hooked dried-blood spatter.
Eyes cling to a Klein-bottle planet in an abyss.

Winter, Washington Square, halcyon days.
Exchanging form, cryptic intent, despair.
A calf-length orange dress even then démodé.

A dahlia blooms dark rose
though chewed by an earwig while a lady bug oversleeps.

Chariots spray dirt and gravel.
A cormorant and widebody jet fly left to right.
Then a boat sails left to right, upstream.
Small wavelets rush downstream with youthful enthusiasm.
They have slightly different shapes.
The clouds are like the Rockies, letting a yellowish light
        ghoulishly pollute the river.

I'm in love with your small breasts, learning how hard
        it is to gaze discreetly.
"Why are you making that face?"
The desperate quarry's heart stops beating.

A fluttering in the sky, a break in the clouds, a hot ray
heats up and burns an acre of earth.
I think I'll just slip away.

Most extra-terrestrials are based on trees.
A reconfiguring plash pricks the past,
a dark past of solemn, deliberate, unrecognized deviance.

We were drowning,
a wall was carpentered where pink phlox praised the Virgin.

City yellow brick, Mediterranean horse-red stone.
Utilities make their marks.

Teal and Gomez-Dep "skirt sierras."
Classical theater thrives.
We have our own shady, dusty faraway style.

"You look like you might know Chinese."

CONSTELLATIONS

The nation of night regenerated.
Archers draw.
I fall asleep up there. Repetitive sails dip and sway.
Hulls mill in injured indecision, shift from foot to foot.
The wedge instantly sticks,
a galaxy's tip is anywhere.

The state's red decks are swabbed, a grapefruit twinkles.

Top and bottom sheets twist, the bottom is pulled away,
it's ten times its uninflated size, it's kissed.
It takes requests and performs with sensual abandon.

I play JD, raise board pierced by rusty nail.
Disk choreographs alarm.

Limping cricket flees mower blades.

MY NAME IS ...

Queen Fog is fed by autumn's earnest nectar.
Sails rock in still air over evenly spaced waves that motor
    relentlessly onshore.
One crown is orange paint, another an oblong cranberry.
Two brown juvenile gulls fly through the vast indoors.

The year's economy is beached on cold sandy soil.
"Dear Sir, please ..." in the languages of crows, grasshoppers,
    and foxes
bursts from microworld alleys. We share a shy child's daring.
Our intention gets completely lost. When we sleep
we join the world of overseers, who don't explore forbidden
    drawers or locked rooms,
whose invertebrate desires bribe dragons.

We've done all we can for now. We look past.
The Mother of Debate tows her blue cloud.

Lead, flame, acid,
scattered creams, a Renaissance corps of earths and grounds,
gold clots, patient, ragged, inditing gravity.

I need repair, renewal, an opera of my name.

The black overcoat closes.
An eager stare at the screen.
It will erupt a thing—
a song—its choir.

It's wet, honey scented, chill.
Severely slowed, sleepy hornets and bees
succumb under vegetable debris,
prolonging a grand past in delirium.

Limbs in rose and yellow tatters plead from behind fences,
never earning sympathy.

Gold volumes wave, flap, slosh in abrupt abridgements of
    impulse.

Fresh mauve clover—masked care-givers.
A representative leaf is archived by eyes.
A warm, yellow-green, frosted bough beats in step with
    my syndrome.
Oases flare up in shadows.
Cloud populations shuffle toward asylum at extremities of
    the peeling Earth.

Speeding through yellow and purple mums,
a relaxed large-leaved death.
It gives up, slows, is revered and feared.

Pimpled stone wall.
Wisdom in barrenness.

Coal bodies in illuminated skirts—
tutus on trees,
crinolines of frost,
leafy brooches.

Expectation-jarring materials appear organic.
Shocking installation placed *en plein air.*
Junk tossed aground.

I might be subsumed in color,
its subatomic-to-cosmologic continuity,
become an autumn color wheel, both soft and spiky,
a folded, twisted, shredded, torn, elegant shape—the eye's
      threat.

What is the Lord's wish?
Speckling, gesturing, journeying.

Shaken off twigs by an alighted sparrow bounced by its perch,
　　a curtain of drops blinks.

Sickly, lavender, late chrysanthemums.

Limbs nearly naked to the crotch, gold ornaments
　　　hung on black.
Individual flecks draw me in.
The particles dismember my understanding.

Stiff, prim, battered lives of oaks shiver in galaxies of glitter,
　　fogs of color.

The sun's a pearl.

A seaside tub full of silver leaves.

Elm merging wrist and "front," the beam of a mind.

Sprigs perched on broken pedestal, a yellow pole hid in
yellow foliage, straight.

Lollipop stick jerked around by sucking lips.

Running gray-pink legs support mid-thigh skirt, pocketed
hands.

High unlaced fresh work boots.

Unlit sumac torches.

It has eyes, usually shut, driven by greed.
Long shadows—spikes meant to impale lain aside.
Light diminishes what's left, lingering forms maintaining
    wandlike poise.

Sweep the exposition floor!
Stanza after stanza pours its plot into sleeping ears.
A flash flood of berries spills down ravines of beams, the more
    sickly colors chagrined.
Clusters shield eyes from sun.

This is an articulation of my deepest values.
That despairing lettered sign, gold smeared in streaked vinyl,
white plastic garden chair, wrinkled paper bag slipping to
    the ground, a disappointed failure of a smile.
A neatly trimmed evergreen shrub is covered with fallen leaves.

My hand pets your hard cheek, your throat.
Our feathers are erect, a song pipes, cheers, and breaks.

Accepting my values is my sole value.
An impasto of crumbled colored media camouflages long
    shadows, which lie broken on the ground.
It might be the physical universe, it might be my eyes, it might
    be my principles and disposition.

A leisurely, principled process, ending in a paragraph of
      decorative observation.
The paragraph is isolated from peripheral energies, themselves
      formal compositions.

The sun is gone, pearling clouds.
What's the source of the beech's grand purpose?

At this moment I don't know if I love or hate this animal.
Purple curtains in a brown house.
Our plans are on the drawing board.
If only we had the chance to explain ourselves!
Better to live on.

Modernism's dead.
A gloomy wand shimmies.
A blue lake among clouds dizzies upside-down humans.
Our heads have been rattled, shattered, slivered.
It's just 20th-century stuff.
Some colorless remnants are shredded on branches,
a maroon sapling leans away from the future.
I thrive in weird climates custom made for me.
The shape of a coif and its outlines are frazzled.
There are few days, few moments left.

Skeletons replace masses.

The world is complex in another way, though not a new one.

Polls indicate considerable despair, considerable hope.

A china-blue falsehood diverts this honeymoon.

My irresistable pain clouds children's eyes and cheeks.

Their imitation is sincere.

Numbers overwhelm.

Mexican, Russian, arctic, and tropical phantoms swarm.

A perpetually blinking light.

Gray pods explode in woolly white clouds, torches in a
    procession of vigilantes.
Lyricism is macerated in drams of poisoned anger.
The relevance of this putty-colored sky is inescapable.

When will the Earth stop being a spiritual realm?

We cross Pinkham St. at a ruminative speed.
Which building in Harvard Square burned last night?

Leafless trees hold their last pose.
They are in thrall and must be redeemed.

A tree crown shaped like a conical rick is still reddish brown
    with leaves.
It's a small philosophical light, hardly enough to read by.
I want to draw that contour, suggest a body.

Vertical orange halogen reflections fade with apparent depth.
Most untwinkling starlike bulbs are aligned one way or
    another.

"Some flowers are good Christians."

Clear beads on braids.
What words—words?—does she sing?
Pale scratchy drizzle lightens dampness-darkened colors.
Plainest coffee-brown house.
Getting through childhood alive.

Can a cloud hide?

Beneath a premonitory sky, imps toss bits of leaves in eyes
    as if they were vials of acid.

Spirits and demons clamor, throng, anticipate being sucked
    across a vacuum by a breathless blade's intake of air.

A droning red-brown glow circles prophetic trees.

Obeying encrypted instructions, frogs ooze into sleep-inducing
   mud.
In the spring, after a lengthy separation, they will be happy
   once again to see me, hopping instead of bowing.

Along the river, pale rime-suffused air obscures ice, which
   echoes the bank's contours less and less sharply as it spreads.
The shrunk evergreens are darker.
Pruned crowns of trees sprout colored lightbulbs.

"I'm taking you with me!" a tenacious icicle shouts, then plunges.
Arms stretch toward the wings.
He can't make the motor start.
The scene is silent, uncanny, colorless, as if recorded using a
   process abandoned before my birth.

I want to believe that I can be the mist.
Being dominant is nothing.
The neighborhood stretches up its twiggy arms.
A black leather jacket. No arms. Leopard-print scarf. Pale lips
    being painted.
The vapor's nation endures.

All the while a sea of floes
a sky of clouds
peaks poking out

This racing heart
conforms to routine
all day

How was
your
weekend?

Mine was
anesthetizing
thank goodness

looking
forward
to dark

I do not have patience
to not rush
out of character
formed a "forever" ago.

'Twould be great to be
oo-ing and ah-ing at
stuff once again, i.e.,
"a gain."

I am merely
a blemished pixel
on the screen.
Turquoise-blue mountains
out the window.

Forever is a long
way off in either
direction.
The surface of the pond erupts.
A plague of hops.

III

RECITATIVE

One peculiarity of the past is that it is irrecoverable. Even
tapes and films can't do it. The past is a seed that continues to
develop after it's gone. Ideas about the past accumulate,
aggregate. Ideas about the past are etched in stone. It gets to
be chaotic. You can't disentangle truth from falsehood.
Witnesses lie for self-serving motives. Historical records are
like fossil skeletons; they can be pieced together in more than
one way and the creature thus created has no personality.
History is porous. I want to return to the past, at least to some
parts of it. I'd like to return to the early forties. I'm
sentimental over you. There was something special about the
thirties. The Great War changed everything. Authors tend to
ignore the underside of society. Certain things were simply not
discussed. Every culture has its blind spot. People in the future
will look back on us with sympathy for our foibles.
I'm embarrassed about some aspects of my youth. Some
people had more to overcome than others. Silent movies are
priceless records of their time. Cleaning up old sound
recordings digitally is a crime. The best arrangement of words
locks in the truth. Wearing cotton is a sensuous link to history.
Wearing leather and fur resurrects the true animal in me.

RESISTANCE IS FUTILE

They will eat anything, even sun.

They drank their whiskey and smoked their cigars.
They wished even more people had been killed.

Undeserving spring arrives only by virtue of a technicality.
I stumble on broken and rotten acorns misplaced by squirrels.
A while ago, I dreamt about horses drowning in a blue-green
    flood.

Though my complete unhappiness doesn't correct its crippled
    plunge, tender leaves charge en masse.
The street is plated with golden pollen.
A small girl kicks a soccer ball and falls on her tush.

They ate it all, leaving us nothing.

Even though we are the most athletic of nations,
our sky shows a totally unmuscular complexion, thin, pale
peaches-and-cream imperfectly hiding a blue breast
        that goes on and on.
Ignoring it is a vain wish.

Haze begins to yield and blush.
Cars squint, calm thickets patter.
Some signs seem shrill—
"Don't block driveway!"

Other things, however, won't be carried further.
Burdens are shed.

Growth neatens itself, fulfills.
More of us are eyesores.
Dig deep for genius.
Low-crotched black tree flees in alarm a crouching shrub's
    mad ecstasy.

Half-red Winston filter half unsmoked.
Red maple flowers on gray branches.

O green delight! Thrusts forward casually,
hits, taps obstacles.

"Move it, Big Boy, loosen up!"

Circular swirls torment the eye.
Playful designs tempt to degeneracy.

EARLY SPRING

Les nuages de Paris vont vite.
Allons!
Blue scilla, Radovan Karadzic, Mariah Carey—mantras that
    earn you a night's rest.
At dawn I wake refreshed by the thrum.

I was at morn disturbed by voices beyond, conspiring 'neath
    my window.
A perfectly braided wisteria vine was broken.
I thrust my head through the leaves to see.
Frogs clogged the bog, loudly caroling. Swamp irises shot up.
Potherbs dripped through foliage.

On a stone bench I sat, 'neath a prune tree in bloom.
Wind blew white petals' false snow.
Planks under the garden echoed 'gainst brick walls hid by a
    painted shrubbery of flats.
An inner and outer flicker 'twixt dark and light
looped and spiraled higher and higher—like a kite.
A swallow inspected me, twittered, flew towards the sun.

BURNING

My father was in charge of the library.
He marched back and forth on sentry duty.
Though the countryside is lush today, it was barren then.
There were a few pruned and sullen trees, and crops, of course.

Are landscapes inheritable?
I leafed through a volume of Civil War photographs.
People either have a job and work hard too many hours
or can't work at all and get poorer and poorer.

Ages of steam and iron and illumination quickly fled.
Violets spread through a neglected patch of lawn.
Some were purple, others mostly white with purple centers,
still others veined with a purple that looked nearly charcoal.

Stands of slim-stemmed peonies.

These flowers at my feet are like care.

Under my feet the turf heals.

Dozens of quick saurians feed in deep lawn.

King Kong rules behind those Egyptian gates.

The zipper on my windbreaker is stuck.

The large pink tulips are out of place.

I told the cat not to swat the bumblebee.

A great blue heron is flushed by a jogger.

The sun is not so large after all. Clouds are larger.

Crows exhale.

Last night I was blotto.

The house we had in 1930 offered a great view of Los Angeles.

Overlapping herringboned leaflets. Red socks.

Every land is an improvisation,
the exotic flowering tree at the edge of the emperor's domain,
that splash, that slash of color that birds vainly try to sew
      into a bale.

A cardinal pecks at violets, an oriole perches in a bronze beech.
A squirrel falls from gigantic willow, startling a spotted
      sandpiper.
Swallows make endless loose vortices.
Grim floating flowers and worm-dangling silk make air
      labyrinthine.

In olden times, when it was, like, wet, even Cretaceous,
a child in olive overalls walked down a dusty street alone.
A widow opened her creaky casements on Jerome Avenue and
    beckoned.
Here's some candy. Run down to the liquor store. Has my
    letter arrived yet?
You are gaping. It is coming at you, but you are stuck there
    in the middle of the street.

Thick moted sunlight pillars stake tilted stonelike trunks.

Nearly empty streets, quietness, the cocker spaniel and the
    collie shuffling along.

There's an effect in the sky
of clouds
There's an effect of speedboats
waking up sailboats
And on the ground a desolate effect
of people thirsting

A lone geranium haircut on a tiny head
An acorn hops across the path
like a Mexican jumping bean
Later on, the acorn's ambitions are definitively squelched

Some blues along the French and Spanish route
Some Southern cooking some Creole cuisine

The goat nibbles at your ankles
You are imprinted on its brain it is fixated
The noisy smoky sidewheeler is coming round the bend

The climate varies to an unknown degree

The clouds are standard-issue baroque.
We are inside one now. Take a look around.

Okay soldier, pick a book and take a seat.

One cloud is actually inside me, booby trapping key
    passageways.

I go overboard in my interests, but I lack "stick-to-itiveness."
I'm listening to Stravinsky (the Cantata), Vivaldi, Brahms,
    and Cibo Matto.

Ultimately, I took *Childe Harold* out of the library.
The wooden card catalogs have been disappeared.

He was gorgeous, the woman at the nursery said. *I swear
    I was "salviating!"*
I laugh as I inscribe the "nomiker."

Her foot is pink, not brown.
Does this mean she's superior to labor?
Her thigh is round, not toned.
Sky fades with pale rain.
Inside the mist, she lifts her crown—
an enormous figure—and smiles.
The trees love her, they're dry,
hissing all summer.
It's early for autumn.
What's within that brain?
The thunder is only now
following shivering flashes,
but it doesn't yet limp away.
Reflections in the greenish window—
so much better than the view.

Things get better, then worse.
This doesn't mean our efforts are futile.
A maple burns from the top down.
Dahlias flop like landed fish.
An ivy's grip fails. The abyss—forget-me-not!—beckons.
Ollie's lavender lettering wakes up the insipid blood.
It's "ostensible" (Lord Byron).
I saw some asters, permitted now.

My hands smell like raw artichokes.
I left clothes on the line at home.
I shall not ingest poisons.

The context never resolves itself in acceptance.
Drugs course through my system.
Let's throw cups and clocks at the wall!

Ash and mucus explode through vents.

I am a *boulevardier* in Paris
My ambition is to study science
Atomic structure
Sex lives
Bridge construction
Everything with a subtext

Then I shall return
An interview
will sum this up
for my successors
The media have confronted the issue
Exoticism
Theater
Hands on hips, decurved bill

Anyway, let's change our method of transportation
Under these circumstances animals look scrawny
The dome and ironwork should be cleaned
Once a week there's a farmers' market on this spot
At this time of day, stare at maps

New repairs, pale green oak,
a point, a fish, a plaid shirt.
Glassy river betrothed to asters.
All still but traffic.
Monstrous button eyes of owl.
A patient blind rider.

More than the corps self-consciously motioning in unison,
     half-remembering its steps,
trees in rows are special objects
unveiling true personalities one by one.
Busby Berkeley style, they divide up into unconvincing
     geometric shapes
or huddle defensively in groups to receive the choreographer's
     notes.

Then we hold a shallow conversation.
You call in the middle of the night to read me Biblical proverbs.
Footprints on the sea persist, are eventually
slurred to the ordinary stuff of rapid sea—melange of scales,
     events between scales.
Whirred away one time, you fall back
     in an orbit slightly out of phase with mine.

Nothing counts.
A bird's nervous flight,
a young oak fated to grow in the stocks of a fence.
Instant tatters, soggy lilac mums.
A juniper spews out its foliage.

She sucks Pepsi through a white straw.
Her vertical curtain of hair brushes a horizontally striped collar.
Foreshortening takes me back to the sixties.
They let me pass, my curlicued penmanship.
Clotted red ornamental maple.

Young Russian artists are "completely harmonical with
    themselves," things have changed so much.
They have no time to define themselves as bad or good.
Their inheritance skipped several generations.
They don't labor under the misapprehension that they are
    what they seem.
They are quick to point out, quick to qualify and to correct.

SELF AND SELF

Thank you for the sea.
It drones.

Frost outlines pale, sugary leaves, *un petit gâteau de campagne.*
I drift and drift for good.

You're a sea, an ocean—perhaps a geometry?—pondering
    resistant thoughts.

A frozen, asymmetrical net in morning's hair.
I fall for driven types, cursèd fate.
Christmas lights blink like a sea, a computer.

Thank you for the sea.
It goes "woo woo."

Can't the Cyclops comb its hair?
A balletic arm of cloud never quite fully extends.
It knows its sadness to be a curse and falls in with the wrong crowd.

A tree clenches its fists and spits an ineffectual epithet.
It stands still as we drift freely.

Thank you for etching a two-dimensional sea in my brain.

Maddened by phantoms, it shakes its locks.

RAGS TO RICHES

It's not reduced but enriched.

About this time the band members had all arrived.

faux
echt

It was good to be concerned at the end of the war, not
        so empty that we descended from
idealism to existentialism and even
lower, to something worse than being an animal.

At least I can respect *them!*
Often they are completely unaware—ignorant, innocent.
They can live in the desert where wind fills their holes with
        sand, then dig themselves out over and over again.

People are hectically mending fences and amending laws.
Dancers in patent leather shoes wear costumes in startling
        yellows and reds tipped and trimmed in black.
The fringed fields of a sect's paradise rouse and ripple.

He bowed graciously when he saw we were speechless in his presence.
One day, finally, we heard what he said about us behind our backs.
Only radio can make this happen.
Our heads are filled with thousands of tunes.

The sun is an empty white stain.

Eyes explore orange gardens asleep,
then other eyes, darting or keen.

Faded flag, mountain of crushed cartons.

Buttery sun's light o'erspreads thatchy thicket.

TO THE SKY

My orange-yellow herb tea warms like the horizon, which
   offers pink as well.

So, you clouds! so *what* that you are quilted here and there?
So *what* that upper and lower layers cross hatch, and it
   feels like a net dropped on my head?
Someone with a headache drapes a dark cloth over my cage to
   make me stop singing by simulating night.

While the river's wavelets idle, you form such long straight
   tracks!
A pigeon makes a foray into your lawless boondocks of
   emptiness.
As far away in the distance as I can see, a silent, violent, icy
   surf crashes.

TULIPS

A familiar alien, a colorless tulip stands blindly in winter's
    debris.

"I hate this girl!"
Lying on a limb that stretches out over the water, she gazes
    upward.
There's a coerced smile, shut off quickly.
I hate this world.

Le parking is full.
A cold wind blows from the east—no, west—through crevices
    and over mounds, on pilgrimage.
Compassionately, it hugs a battered silver maple.

Headset and leather *de rigueur* in *le cockpit.*
The hat is *prêt-à-porter.*

Jumbo jet tulip in baby pink coat.

A HAZE, BOATS

On a good day in May my body learns.
Only a few meetings, hopeful for others or to avoid some.
Is what I'm getting at obvious?
I think I'm being tracked or harassed.

I reluctantly agree that I'm too twisted, that I should reform.
Sirens lure me outdoors to the swings.
Did Richard think I slept with her?
Misunderstandings grow great, fingers trail in water.

In the real world, difficult projects are accomplished with
        matter-of-fact ease.
Going directly to the source of anguish—the senses—to tear
        down, always to tear down.
I'm ready to learn.
No, I'm not.

I don't consider myself an American.
It's sort of like the three-body problem.
There's almost nothing worth watching here and I need
        something to watch.
Benignly complex personal relationships.

My life is a paradox, many discarded shells.
Oak tassels cling to tennis balls.
"*Ocho? Seis?*" Tennis ball numbers in Spanish.
Are they pilgrims? What shrine?

BIFOCALS

Today I can't see anything two feet in front of me.
Big floppy flakes float to the ground at the Louvre.
All this grand architecture is at its best in gruesome weather.

You have a mean alligator tooth, arms boneless as a newt's.
Your hands are acrobats in embroidered Schiaparelli costumes.
At each ray, the web is tugged firmly by a spinneret.

We drank that yellow-green piss by the quart.
I found a book that describes a time when people were
    normally cranky.
The corn and melons came in fine. We're considering adding
    peas and potatoes next year.

You were much more interesting when your persona was
    mysterious.
Two old river birches, shaggy and blemished, are mysterious
    like that.
Shiny toothed arrows attenuate to a bearded wispy tip
    swaying on long dusty limbs, a frottage-like blotter
    effect, invisible in silhouette.

Then, of course, horrible things happened.
A hornet and dragonfly clung together in deadly combat on a
    milkweed leaf, a sparrow rushed at an orange butterfly,
    an aging pit bull shook a squirrel trapped in its jaws.
A higher education helped me to acquire my love of farming.

SONNET

The weather's beginning to fall apart.
As if not opaque enough, my cards hint at a cloudy life.

I like the unease in your bony hands.
The music is "excellent" but possibly unimportant.
I bet I can guess what kind of car you drive.

The clouds are waffled. They button blue sides.
Your wrinkled ochre shirt came right from the laundry,
overused eyes pestered by strands of hair falling in the way.
How much we overlap I can't decide.

Pink and blue leaf hoppers, a sixties insect, munch sunflower
    rays.
Dragonflies, courtesy of M. Eiffel, are brighter than crystal
    palaces.
I sip from solitude's diversionary clarity.

Sit side by side, elbows on the counter.
Efface this memory with "a brush of the sponge."